P9-ELG-340

CH

TODAY'S ★★ NAVY ★★★★ HEROES

by Jessica Rudolph

Consultant: Fred Pushies
U.S. SOF Adviser

BEARPORT
PUBLISHING

New York, New York

Credits

Cover and Title Page, © Jake Warga/Corbis and © Stocktrek/Getty Images; 4, © Greg Martin/SuperStock; 5, © U.S. Navy/SIPA/Newscom; 6, © U.S. Marine Corps/Cpl. Seth Maggard; 7, © U.S. Marine Corps/Cpl. Seth Maggard; 8T, © U.S. Navy/Hospital Corpsman 2nd Class Wayne Nelms; 8B, © AP Photo/Jacob Silberberg; 9L, © Mujahed Mohammed/AFP/Getty Images; 9R, © Eric Feferberg/AFP/Newscom; 10, © AP Photo/Kevin Frayer; 11L, © U.S. Marine Corps/ LCPL Nathan L. Barnes; 11R, © Charlie Neuman/San Diego Union-Tribune/ Zuma Press/Newscom; 12T, © U.S. Navy/Mr. Bill W. Love; 12B, © U.S. Marine Corps/Cpl Brian M. Henner; 13, © Louie Palu/ZUMA Press/Newscom; 14, © Photo provided by Richard S. Lowry, author of New Dawn: The Battles for Fallujah; 15, © AP Photo/Caller Times, George Gongora; 16T, © Chief Petty Officer Terry Leeper; 16B, © Chief Petty Officer Terry Leeper; 17, © Chief Petty Officer Terry Leeper; 18, © Chief Petty Officer Terry Leeper; 19L, © Sean M Haffey/ZUMA Press/Newscom; 19R, © GSgt. Mark Oliva/DOD/ZUMA Press/Newscom; 20T, © U.S. Marine Corps; 20B, © AP Photo/Khalid Mohammed; 21, © Katie Callan; 22T, © U.S. Navy/Photo courtesy Monsoor family; 22B, © AP Photo; 23, © U.S. Navy/Mass Communication Specialist Brian Aho; 24T, © U.S. Navy; 24B, © U.S. Navy; 25, © Chuck Liddy/Raleigh News & Observer/MCT/Landov; 26, © AP Photo/ Pat Wellenbach; 27, © Jim Bourg/Reuters/Landov; 28T, © Dr. Heidi Kraft; 28B, © U.S. Navy photo by Mr. Oscar Sosa; 29T, © Defense Department Photo; 29B, © U.S. Navy/Gary Nichols 31, © Keith McIntyre/Shutterstock.

Publisher: Kenn Goin
Senior Editor: Lisa Wiseman
Creative Director: Spencer Brinker
Design: Dawn Beard Creative
Photo Researcher: Picture Perfect Professionals, LLC

Library of Congress Cataloging-in-Publication Data

Rudolph, Jessica.
  Today's Navy heroes / by Jessica Rudolph ; consultant, Fred Pushies.
    p. cm. — (Acts of courage: inside America's military)
  Includes bibliographical references and index.
  Audience: Ages 7-12.
  ISBN-13: 978-1-61772-446-6 (library binding)
  ISBN-10: 1-61772-446-7 (library binding)
  1. United States. Navy—Biography—Juvenile literature. 2. Iraq War, 2003—Juvenile literature. 3. Afghan War, 2001—Juvenile literature. I. Pushies, Fred J., 1952- II. Title.
  V62.R84 2012
  956.7044'345092273—dc23
                    2011040259

For more information, write to Bearport Publishing Company, Inc., 45 West 21st Street, Suite 3B, New York, New York 10010. Printed in the United States of America.

10 9 8 7 6 5 4 3 2 1

★★★ Contents ★★★

September 11 4

At War with Iraq 6

The Battle of Al-Nasiriyah 8

Bullets and Rockets 10

By Boat, by Foot 12

"Doc's Hit!" 14

A Secret Attack 16

Standing His Ground 18

Helping Others 20

The Hardest Decision 22

Fighting the Taliban 24

True Heroes 26

More Navy Heroes 28

Glossary 30

Bibliography 31

Read More 31

Learn More Online 31

Index 32

About the Author 32

September 11

September 11, 2001, started out as a beautiful, clear day in New York City. People hurried to work in the bright sunshine. At 8:46 that morning, however, everything changed. An airplane going more than 450 miles per hour (724 kph) slammed into the North Tower of the World Trade Center. Seventeen minutes later, a second plane crashed into the South Tower. Smoke poured from the massive buildings and flames shot out of the top floors.

The North and the South Towers, called the Twin Towers, after the plane crashed into the North Tower on September 11, 2001

About two hours after being hit by the planes, both towers collapsed.

Later that day, the U.S. government learned that the two planes had been **hijacked** by members of a **terrorist group** called **Al Qaeda**. New York City, however, was not the only place that was attacked on September 11. Al Qaeda terrorists had also hijacked two other planes. They flew one into the **Pentagon** in Virginia, and the other one crashed into a field in Pennsylvania. In all, nearly 3,000 people died. Al Qaeda's leader, Osama bin Laden, had organized the attack on the United States from his base in Afghanistan. To destroy the terrorists' training camps and find bin Laden, the U.S. government sent troops to Afghanistan in October 2001.

U.S. Navy sailors in Afghanistan

At War with Iraq

Less than two years later, in 2003, the U. S. war against terrorism expanded to Iraq. Some government officials believed that Saddam Hussein, the ruler of Iraq, was trying to build powerful weapons, including **nuclear** ones, to use against the United States and other countries. They thought he needed to be stopped. On March 20, 2003, the United States sent military troops to invade Iraq. Though weapons were never found, the United States and its **allies** were able to remove Saddam Hussein from power.

U.S. Navy sailors in Iraq

○ **Some of the places where Navy sailors have served in Afghanistan and Iraq**

Thousands of brave men and women served in Afghanistan and Iraq in the years following September 11, 2001. This book recounts some of the acts of courage by U.S. Navy sailors who have fought in these wars. The bravery and selflessness they have shown in fighting for their country is the very definition of *hero*.

A Navy sailor on patrol

The Navy is the branch of the **armed forces** responsible for military operations on the seas.

The Battle of Al-Nasiriyah

Luis Fonseca

Rank:	Hospital Apprentice (Later promoted to Petty Officer Second Class)
Hometown:	Fayetteville, North Carolina
Conflict:	Iraq War
Date:	March 23, 2003
Honor:	Navy Cross

In March 2003, Navy **Corpsman** Luis Fonseca found himself in one of the first major battles of the Iraq War. He was traveling with a group of **Marines** in a **convoy** consisting of 12 giant amtracks. The Marines' mission was to capture a bridge from enemy forces in the city of Al-Nasiriyah.

Amtracks can carry troops on both land and through water. Each one can transport more than 20 Marines at a time.

When the convoy approached the bridge, enemy fighters launched a huge attack. From inside his amtrack, Fonseca heard bullets bouncing off the vehicle. Suddenly, he got a call over the radio from his commander—an amtrack had been hit by a **rocket-propelled grenade** (RPG). Fonseca knew the Marines inside the vehicle would need his help.

The corpsman grabbed his medical bag, left his amtrack, and raced up the road. The damaged amtrack was in flames. Along with some of the Marines, Fonseca helped drag five injured men from the blazing vehicle. Some of the wounded had **shrapnel** sticking out of their bodies. Two Marines had each lost part of a leg in the blast.

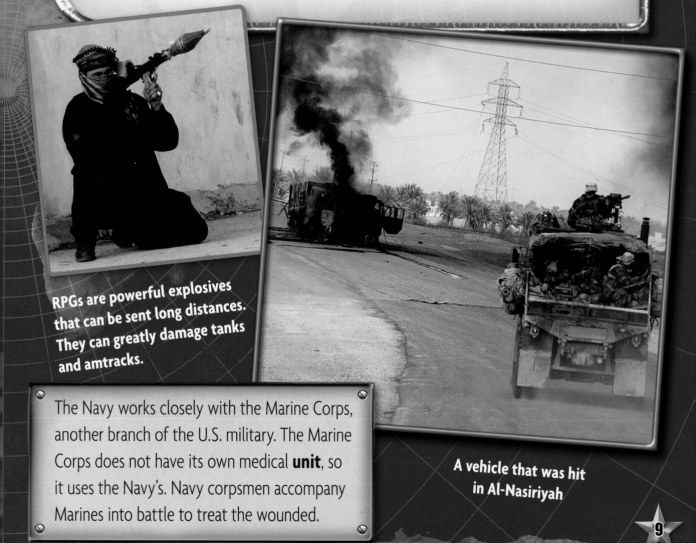

RPGs are powerful explosives that can be sent long distances. They can greatly damage tanks and amtracks.

The Navy works closely with the Marine Corps, another branch of the U.S. military. The Marine Corps does not have its own medical **unit**, so it uses the Navy's. Navy corpsmen accompany Marines into battle to treat the wounded.

A vehicle that was hit in Al-Nasiriyah

Bullets and Rockets

Bullets and rockets flew around Fonseca as he quickly performed first aid on the injured men. Fonseca was sure he would be killed, but he stayed focused.

Once Fonseca had treated the men, he directed some of the uninjured Marines to move four of them to another amtrack. As Fonseca tried to move the fifth one, the enemy fire became even more intense. He couldn't safely reach the amtrack that the Marines had carried the other men to. So, with the wounded Marine on his back, he ran to a nearby ditch for cover. About ten minutes later, Fonseca flagged down a military truck, which took the two men to safety.

Soldiers often carry the wounded over their shoulders. This makes it easier to carry someone for longer distances.

The five Marines who Fonseca had helped that day were taken to a nearby hospital. They all survived. For the brave corpsman, the battle was terrifying. However, his job was not to worry about his safety, but the safety of the Marines around him.

The Navy Cross

On August 11, 2004, at a ceremony at Camp Lejeune, North Carolina, Luis Fonseca received the Navy Cross for his heroism. This award is the second-highest medal given to members of the Navy and Marines, after the Medal of Honor.

Luis Fonseca had been in Iraq for only about three days when the battle of Al-Nasiriyah took place.

By Boat, by Foot

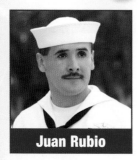

Juan Rubio

Rank:	Hospital Corpsman Third Class (Later promoted to Hospital Corpsman Second Class)
Hometown:	San Angelo, Texas
Conflict:	Iraq War
Date:	January 1, 2005
Honor:	Silver Star and Purple Heart

Juan Rubio is another Navy corpsman who knows what it's like to put other people's safety first. In 2005, Rubio was on a boat **patrol** with a Marine unit on the Euphrates River in Iraq. When the group reached the small town of Haditha, they went in search of **insurgents**.

Marines patrolling the Euphrates River

Rubio and the Marines didn't know it, but enemy fighters had hidden an **IED** in a large metal can placed against a wall near the area that they were searching. As they walked past the container, the bomb exploded. The fiery blast pushed a Marine into Rubio, throwing the corpsman against a building. He fell to the ground, **unconscious**.

When the corpsman regained consciousness a few seconds later, he saw bullets hitting the dirt around him. He was in the middle of a raging battle! Rubio looked around and saw that some of the Marines near him had been injured. Without worrying about his own safety, Rubio crawled over to the wounded and began giving them medical treatment.

Insurgents sometimes bury IEDs in the roads American troops drive on, or hide them in objects American soldiers walk near. When the troops get close enough to the hidden bomb, the enemy sets it off by remote control.

"Doc's Hit!"

As the gunfire continued, Rubio and the Marines carried the injured men back to the boats. The group raced a mile and a half (2.4 km) upstream to waiting trucks. The vehicles would take the injured back to **base**, where they could get more care.

Juan Rubio in Iraq

Corpsmen are trained to give medical care. Even though they are not doctors, the Marines have given them the nickname "Doc."

Most people would have been glad to flee a dangerous battle, but not Rubio. He wanted to hurry back to fight the insurgents. However, after dropping off the wounded, one of the Marines spotted blood on the corpsman's leg. Rubio thought it was from treating the injured. The Marine shouted, "No, Doc, your pants are ripped and I can see it. Doc's hit!" In all the commotion, Rubio hadn't noticed that he had shrapnel buried in his leg from the IED.

Rubio reluctantly agreed to get medical treatment. However, he refused to return to the United States for more medical care. A day and a half after his injury, he was back with his unit.

On April 27, 2006, Juan Rubio received the Silver Star for his heroism. This is the Navy's third-highest award for courage in battle. Rubio also received the Purple Heart, which is given to soldiers who are wounded or killed while serving their country. Here, he hugs his children at the ceremony in Corpus Christi, Texas.

A Secret Attack

James Hamill

Rank:	Petty Officer Second Class (Later promoted to Petty Officer First Class)
Hometown:	Wilmington, Delaware
Conflict:	War in Afghanistan
Date:	February 20, 2007
Honor:	Bronze Star with Valor and Purple Heart

Not all members of the Navy encounter the enemy while on patrol. Petty Officer Second Class James Hamill, a Navy photographer, came across the enemy while taking photos at the opening of a new hospital emergency room for the Afghan people in the city of Khost. On that day, in February 2007, about 100 **civilians** came to the outdoor ceremony. Afghan police and American troops surrounded the crowd to protect them from a possible insurgent attack.

Hamill posed for a picture with a few Afghan children just before the ceremony started.

During the ceremony, an American soldier spotted a man with a bomb strapped to his chest running toward the crowd. The soldier lunged toward the **suicide bomber** and tackled him to the ground.

From a few feet away, Hamill watched the struggle. When the bomber broke free and ran closer to the crowd, Hamill knew he had to do something. He couldn't let the terrorist get any closer.

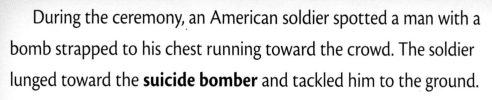

The ceremony for the new hospital

The suicide bomber had tried to get through security by wearing a white coat in order to look like a doctor. When Afghan police tried to stop him for questioning, the terrorist started running away from them toward the crowd gathered outside the hospital.

Standing His Ground

Hamill stepped right in front of the bomber, dropped his camera, and raised his rifle—shooting the bomber several times. As the terrorist fell to the ground, he triggered the bomb.

Army Corporal Anthony Rush remembers what happened after the blast. "People were running everywhere, and it was difficult at first to figure out what was happening," he said. The blast instantly killed the bomber and injured many people, including Hamill, whose stomach was pierced with sharp pieces of shrapnel.

Because the explosion was far enough away, there was little damage to the hospital building where the ceremony took place.

Even if a sailor's main job isn't to fight in combat, he or she is still trained to use a weapon.

Hamill ignored his injury and, because he knew first aid, began to treat those who had even worse injuries than his own. Fortunately, everyone who was injured survived. If not for Hamill's bravery, the suicide bomber could have set off the explosion right in the middle of the crowd. It would have killed many people and destroyed the hospital.

For his heroism, James Hamill received a Bronze Star with Valor (left). When awarded for bravery, it's the fourth-highest combat award of the U.S. Armed Forces. He also received a Purple Heart (right) for the shrapnel wounds he suffered in the explosion.

Helping Others

Nathaniel Leoncio

Rank:	Hospital Corpsman Third Class
Hometown:	Temecula, California
Conflict:	Iraq War
Date:	October 4, 2005
Honor:	Bronze Star with Valor and Purple Heart

Like James Hamill, Hospital Corpsman Third Class Nathaniel Leoncio saved the lives of others while injured. In 2005 in Ramadi, Iraq, the corpsman was on patrol with a Marine unit. As the convoy of Humvees made its way down the road, an IED erupted, flipping over Leoncio's vehicle and pinning him underneath. Marines from the other Humvees heard Leoncio screaming for help and rushed to the scene. Corporal Neil Frustaglio lifted the vehicle just enough so Leoncio could drag his body free.

A Humvee is a large jeep-like military vehicle. Although some Humvees are protected with armor, they can still be destroyed by explosives.

The corpsman's right leg was badly injured. He was in horrible pain and losing blood fast. Yet, unbelievably, he stayed calm while he told the Marines how to apply a **tourniquet** to his leg. Then he guided the Marines in caring for the other injured men. To help his commander, who had shrapnel wounds, Leoncio even painfully rolled over onto his own injured leg to get bandages that were in his back pocket. Leoncio refused to go to the hospital until all the other wounded men were **stable**.

Nathaniel Leoncio's injuries were so bad that his right leg had to be replaced with an artificial one. Today, he is able to walk, surf, and do many other activities.

Nathaniel Leoncio received a Bronze Star with **Valor** and a Purple Heart at a ceremony at Camp Pendleton, in California, on April 6, 2006.

The Hardest Decision

Michael Monsoor

Rank: Master-At-Arms Second Class (Sea, Air and Land)

Hometown: Garden Grove, California

Conflict: Iraq War

Date: September 29, 2006

Honor: Medal of Honor and Purple Heart

While all Navy heroes act courageously, some do so even when they know their actions will likely lead to death. In September 2006, Michael Monsoor, a **Navy SEAL sniper**, was with three other SEALs on a building rooftop in the city of Ramadi, Iraq. They were on the lookout for insurgents on the streets below.

Some of the worst violence of the Iraq War has occurred in Ramadi.

After a few hours, Monsoor felt something hit his chest. An insurgent had thrown a hand grenade at the SEALs. It bounced off Monsoor and landed on the roof. It would explode at any second. Even though he was standing next to the only exit and could have escaped, Monsoor shouted, "Grenade!" Then, without hesitation, he covered the explosive with his body just before it blew up. Monsoor's body shielded his fellow SEALs from the main force of the blast. He was killed, but his amazing valor saved the other men.

Sally and George Monsoor, Michael's parents, accepted the Medal of Honor on their son's behalf from President George W. Bush at a White House ceremony on April 8, 2008. The Medal of Honor is the highest award given by the U.S. military.

The three other SEAL snipers were injured in the explosion and immediately taken to a battlefield hospital. One SEAL, who had shrapnel wounds in his legs, said that Monsoor "never took his eye off the grenade." He added, "He undoubtedly saved mine and the other SEALs' lives, and we owe him."

Fighting the Taliban

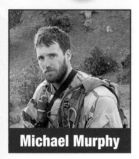

Michael Murphy

Rank:	Lieutenant
Hometown:	Patchogue, New York
Conflict:	War in Afghanistan
Date:	June 28, 2005
Honor:	Medal of Honor and Purple Heart

Michael Monsoor isn't the only SEAL who **sacrificed** his life helping others. In 2005, Navy SEAL Lieutenant Michael Murphy was leading a group that included three other SEALs: Petty Officers Matthew Axelson, Danny Dietz, and Marcus Luttrell. The group was tracking a terrorist leader in the rugged mountains of eastern Afghanistan.

Suddenly, the team's worst nightmare came true when more than 30 armed **Taliban** fighters swarmed over the mountaintop. The enemy fighters surrounded the team and unleashed a storm of gunfire. The four SEALs took cover behind rocks and hills as they shot back.

Lieutenant Michael Murphy and Petty Officers Danny Dietz (left), Marcus Luttrell (center), and Matthew Axelson (right) were able to shoot and kill many Taliban fighters that day.

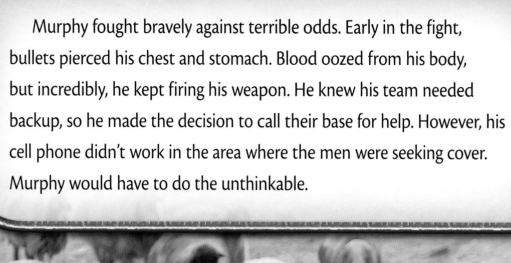

Murphy fought bravely against terrible odds. Early in the fight, bullets pierced his chest and stomach. Blood oozed from his body, but incredibly, he kept firing his weapon. He knew his team needed backup, so he made the decision to call their base for help. However, his cell phone didn't work in the area where the men were seeking cover. Murphy would have to do the unthinkable.

The only civilians the team saw that day in the mountains were three **goatherds**. Marcus Luttrell believes they most likely told local Taliban fighters about the Navy SEALs' location.

True Heroes

Without hesitation, Murphy walked over to an area where his cell phone would work. However, this location made him an easy target for enemy fighters. They aimed at Murphy as he shouted into the phone, "My guys are dying out here . . . we need help." When a bullet hit Murphy's back, he slumped forward and dropped the phone. Remarkably, he picked it up and finished the call. Afterward, he raised his rifle and continued fighting.

Unfortunately, Murphy died from his wounds soon after. When the two-hour fight was over, Axelson and Dietz also lay dead. Only Luttrell escaped and survived.

For his bravery and courage, Michael Murphy was awarded the Medal of Honor. On October 22, 2007, President Bush presented the medal to Murphy's parents, Daniel and Maureen, at a White House ceremony. The U.S. Navy also named one of its warships (shown here) after Murphy.

After Murphy's call for help, a helicopter was sent to rescue the SEALs. However, the insurgents shot it down. Everyone on board was killed.

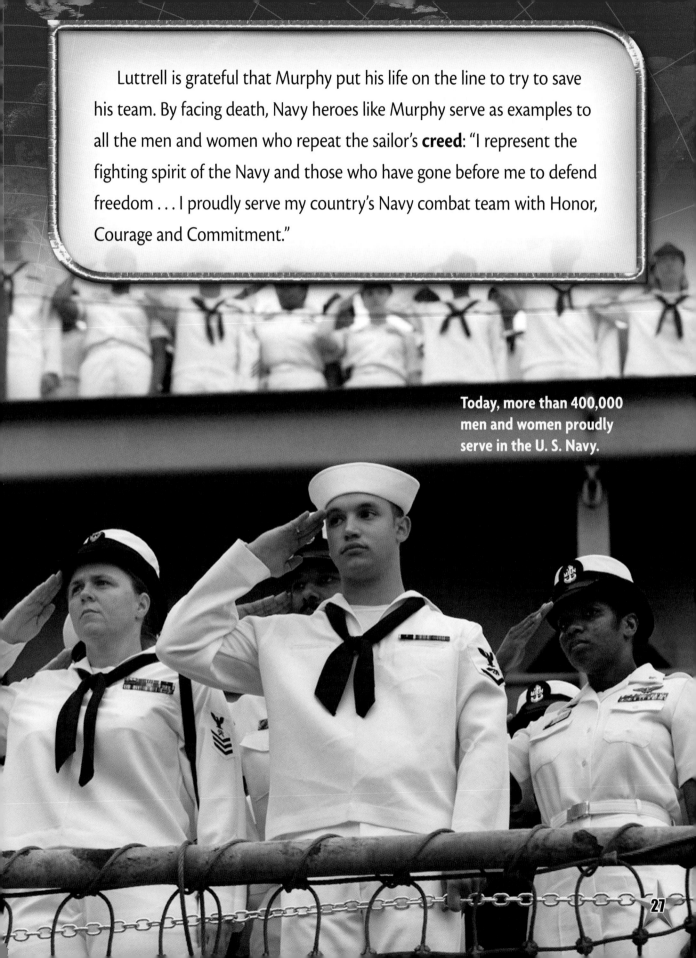

Luttrell is grateful that Murphy put his life on the line to try to save his team. By facing death, Navy heroes like Murphy serve as examples to all the men and women who repeat the sailor's **creed**: "I represent the fighting spirit of the Navy and those who have gone before me to defend freedom . . . I proudly serve my country's Navy combat team with Honor, Courage and Commitment."

Today, more than 400,000 men and women proudly serve in the U. S. Navy.

More Navy Heroes

Here are a few U.S. Navy sailors who have performed heroic acts away from combat.

★ Lieutenant Commander Heidi Kraft ★

Heidi Kraft

In 2004, Lieutenant Commander Heidi Kraft was working as a doctor in a hospital in Iraq. One day, a Marine named Jason Dunham was brought in because he had a major brain injury. He had been wounded while saving other Marines and was now unconscious. Doctors did not expect him to survive. Kraft wanted someone to be with him in his last moments. So she held his hand and told Dunham everyone was proud of him. Unexpectedly, Dunham showed signs of improvement. He squeezed Kraft's hand and moved his head and feet. Since he was making progress, his doctors decided that he was ready for surgery. Unfortunately, Dunham never woke up from the surgery and passed away. Deb Dunham, Jason's mother, was grateful that Kraft took care of her son. She invited Kraft to attend Jason's Medal of Honor ceremony in January 2007. "It stands alone as the single proudest day of my life," Kraft said.

Medal of Honor

⭐ Senior Chief Petty Officer Ralph Chavez ⭐

In 2006, Chief Petty Officer Ralph Chavez took part in a mission to rebuild communities in Afghanistan. He managed 20 construction projects to build water wells, schools, and houses. He also worked to provide health care for more than 3,000 people in 50 villages. Chavez believes his work builds trust between American troops and the Afghan people. "The locals welcomed us into their homes, shared their food, and we got to hear their stories," he said. "It was very rewarding." Chavez received the Bronze Star for his service in Afghanistan.

Ralph Chavez

⭐ Senior Chief Hospital Corpsman Reginald Dean ⭐

Usually, Senior Chief Hospital Corpsman Reginald Dean's job was to train Iraqi soldiers in combat medicine. The corpsman rarely left the safety of Fort Tal Afar. That changed on April 12, 2005. On that day, Dean heard about a suicide car bombing on a nearby road, and he quickly headed to the scene. Once there, Dean saw several wounded Iraqis, including two young children with head injuries. The corpsman rode with them in an ambulance back to the fort. "I held my body over them in case we got shot," said Dean. "They were crying and they were scared . . . I told them everything was okay." In June 2006, Dean received a Bronze Star for giving medical aid to the children as well as to ten other Iraqi civilians.

Reginald Dean after receiving the Bronze Star

Glossary

allies (AL-eyez) friends or supporters

Al Qaeda (AHL KAY-duh) the terrorist group that was responsible for the September 11 attacks on the United States

armed forces (ARMD FORSS-iz) the military groups a country uses to protect itself; in the United States these are the Army, the Navy, the Air Force, the Marines, and the Coast Guard

base (BAYSS) the place soldiers live in or operate from

civilians (si-VIL-yuhnz) people who are not in the military

convoy (KON-voi) a group of military vehicles traveling together for safety

corpsman (KOR-man) an enlisted person who works as a hospital assistant or who accompanies combat troops into battle to give first aid and help the wounded get to safety

creed (KREED) a statement of beliefs

goatherds (GOHT-hurdz) people who tend goats

hijacked (HYE-jackt) illegally took control of by force

IED (ay-ee-DEE) improvised explosive device; a homemade bomb, often set off by remote control

insurgents (in-SUR-juhnts) people who fight against a lawful government or lawful leaders

Marines (muh-REENZ) members of the U.S. Marine Corps who are trained to fight on land, at sea, and in the air

Navy SEAL (NAY-vee SEEL) a sailor in the U.S. Navy who is specially trained to fight at sea, in the air, and on land

nuclear (NOO-klee-ur) having to do with a dangerous type of energy that produces radiation

patrol (puh-TROHL) a walk or drive around an area to guard it and keep watch on people

Pentagon (PEN-tuh-gon) the five-sided building in Virginia that serves as the headquarters of the U.S. Department of Defense

rocket-propelled grenade (ROK-it-pru-PELD gruh-NAYD) a weapon often used by insurgents to damage or destroy buildings or vehicles

sacrificed (SAK-ruh-fyest) gave up something important for a good reason

shrapnel (SHRAP-nuhl) pieces of metal from an exploded bomb or other device

sniper (SNIPE-ur) a rifleman who fires from a concealed place at enemy fighters

stable (STAY-buhl) safe and secure

suicide bomber (SOO-uh-*side* BOM-ur) a person who carries out an attack by blowing up a bomb attached to his or her body

Taliban (TAL-uh-ban) a military and political group that ruled Afghanistan from 1996 to 2001 and remains a strong force in the country

terrorist group (TER-ur-ist GROOP) people who use violence and terror to get what they want

tourniquet (TUR-nuh-ket) a tight bandage wrapped around a limb to lessen the bleeding from a wound

unconscious (uhn-KON-shuhss) not awake; unable to think, hear, feel, or see

unit (YOO-nit) a group or division in the armed forces

valor (VAL-ur) courage and bravery

Bibliography

Larson, Major Chuck, ed. *Heroes Among Us: Firsthand Accounts of Combat from America's Most Decorated Warriors in Iraq and Afghanistan.* New York: New American Library (2008).

Luttrell, Marcus, and Patrick Robinson. *Lone Survivor: The Eyewitness Account of Operation Redwing and the Lost Heroes of Seal Team 10.* New York: Little, Brown and Company (2007).

ourmilitaryheroes.defense.gov/

www.navy.mil/swf/index.asp

Read More

David, Jack. *Navy SEALs.* Minneapolis, MN: Bellwether Media (2009).

Goldish, Meish. *Navy: Civilian to Sailor (Becoming a Soldier).* New York: Bearport Publishing (2011).

Souter, Gerry, and Janet Souter. *War in Afghanistan and Iraq: The Daily Life of the Men and Women Serving in Afghanistan and Iraq.* London, UK: Carlton Books (2011).

Yomtov, Nel. *Navy SEALs in Action (Special Ops).* New York: Bearport Publishing (2008).

Learn More Online

To learn more about today's Navy heroes, visit
www.bearportpublishing.com/ActsofCourage

Index

Afghanistan 5, 6–7, 16, 24
Al-Nasiriyah, Iraq 6, 8–9, 11
Al Qaeda 5
amtracks 8–9, 10
Axelson, Matthew 24, 26

bin Laden, Osama 5
Bronze Star 16, 19, 20–21, 29

Chavez, Ralph 29
civilians 16, 25, 29
corpsmen 8–9, 11, 12–13, 14–15, 20–21, 29

Dean, Reginald 29
Dietz, Danny 24, 26

Fonseca, Luis 8–9, 10–11
Fort Tal Afar 6, 29

Haditha, Iraq 6, 12
Hamill, James 16–17, 18–19, 20
Humvees 20
Hussein, Saddam 6

improvised explosive devices (IEDs) 13, 15, 20
Iraq 6–7, 8, 12, 20, 22

Khost, Afghanistan 6, 16
Kraft, Heidi 28

Leoncio, Nathaniel 20–21
Luttrell, Marcus 24–25, 26–27

Marines 8–9, 10–11, 12–13, 14–15, 20–21, 28
Medal of Honor 11, 22–23, 24, 26, 28
Monsoor, Michael 22–23, 24
Murphy, Michael 24–25, 26–27

Navy Cross 8, 11
Navy SEALs 22–23, 24–25, 26

patrols 7, 12, 16, 20
Pentagon 5
Purple Heart 12, 15, 16, 19, 20, 22, 24

Ramadi, Iraq 6, 20, 22
Rubio, Juan 12–13, 14–15

September 11 4–5, 7
Silver Star 12, 15

About the Author

Jessica Rudolph lives in Phoenix, Arizona. She has edited and written many children's books about history, geography, science, and nature.